Special thanks to our adviser:
Susan Kesselring, M.A., Literacy Educator
Rosemount–Apple Valley–Eagan (Minnesota) School District

Three Presidents Died on the Fourth of July

and Other Freaky Facts About the First 25 Presidents

by **Barbara Seuling**
illustrated by **Matthew Skeens**

PICTURE WINDOW BOOKS
Minneapolis, Minnesota

Editor's Note: This book is about the first 25 men who became president of the United States. The table of contents lists 26 presidents because Grover Cleveland was president for two non-consecutive terms.

Editor: Christianne Jones
Designer: Abbey Fitzgerald
Page Production: Melissa Kes
Art Director: Nathan Gassman
The illustrations in this book were created digitally.

Picture Window Books
5115 Excelsior Boulevard
Suite 232
Minneapolis, MN 55416
877-845-8392
www.picturewindowbooks.com

Library of Congress Cataloging-in-Publication Data
Seuling, Barbara.
Three presidents died on the Fourth of July : and other freaky facts about the first 25 presidents / by Barbara Seuling ; illustrated by Matthew Skeens.
p. cm. — (Freaky facts)
Includes index.
ISBN-13: 978-1-4048-3748-5 (library binding)
ISBN-10: 1-4048-3748-5 (library binding)
1. Presidents—United States—Biography—Miscellanea—Juvenile literature. 2. Presidents—United States—History—Miscellanea—Juvenile literature. 3. Curiosities and wonders—United States—History—Miscellanea—Juvenile literature. I. Skeens, Matthew. II. Title.
E176.1.S5 2007
973.09'9—dc22
2007004026

Table of Contents

George Washington
(1789-1797)

George Washington had lost nearly all of his own teeth by the age of 57. During Washington's endless search for comfortable false teeth, a French dentist made him a set from carved rhinoceros ivory.

The United States had a vice president before it had a president. John Adams was sworn in as vice president nine days before George Washington was sworn in as the first president.

Washington's second inaugural address was the shortest in history. It was just 135 words.

Washington did not want the capital named after him. He preferred Federal City. The city's name was quickly switched after Washington died.

John Adams
(1797-1801)

John Adams knew seven different languages.

The Adams family was the nation's first "First Family" to live in what is now known as the White House.

On his arrival in Washington, Adams found the White House in rough shape. A swamp and a forest surrounded the outside of the house. Inside, only six rooms were ready to live in. The main stairs weren't even finished.

Once, on their way back to the White House, Abigail and John Adams got lost in the woods of Washington, D.C.

John Adams didn't want to be called Mr. President. Instead, he wanted to be called His Highness because it sounded more important.

Adams' favorite horse was named Cleopatra.

5

Thomas Jefferson
(1801-1809)

★★

Thomas Jefferson believed that he stayed healthy by soaking his feet in cold water every morning.

Jefferson's grandson, James Madison Randolph, was the first baby born in the White House.

Jefferson was a skilled violinist.

★★

At receptions, President Jefferson greeted people with a handshake. He felt it was more democratic than the bow from the waist, which was used by Washington and Adams.

After the burning of the Library of Congress in the War of 1812, Thomas Jefferson's personal library was bought by the U.S. government to start a new library.

Jefferson understood Italian, Spanish, French, German, Latin, and Greek.

Jefferson was the first president to have his inauguration in Washington, D.C.

Jefferson's vice president, Aaron Burr, was indicted for murder. He had killed Alexander Hamilton, the nation's first secretary of treasury and Burr's political enemy, in a duel in 1805.

If it was up to Jefferson, the White House would have been red and made out of brick.

Lewis and Clark brought back grizzly bears from their western expedition and presented them to Jefferson as gifts. He kept them in cages on the White House grounds.

James Madison
(1809-1817)

James Madison was the first president to wear long trousers instead of knee breeches.

Madison is known as the "Father of the Constitution" because he led the writing of the important document.

James Madison was the smallest president. He was just 5 feet, 4 inches (163 cm) tall and weighed less than 100 pounds (45 kg).

Dolley Madison was 17 years younger and several inches taller than her husband.

Dolley gave lavish dinner parties. She served many delicacies. Some historians say she introduced ice cream to the United States. After she served it at one of her parties, it became popular.

Friends called Madison by his nickname, "Jemmy."

James Monroe
(1817–1825)

James Monroe was one of the three presidents who died on the Fourth of July. Thomas Jefferson and John Adams were the other two.

Only one foreign country—Liberia—has a capital city named after a U.S. president. The capital is Monrovia, named after James Monroe.

When Monroe ran for re-election in 1820, he was virtually unopposed. A single dissenting vote was cast on purpose, to be sure that George Washington remained the country's only president elected unanimously.

After he left the White House, Monroe was broke. He had to move in with his daughter.

John Quincy Adams (1825-1829)

John Quincy Adams was a great speaker. In fact, he could speak in seven languages.

Adams was the only president to have a foreign-born wife. Louisa was born in England.

As president, Adams rose early to write in his diary. On warm days, he liked to slip down to the Potomac River behind the White House and skinny-dip. One day a reporter surprised him. She sat on his clothes and refused to go away until he promised to give her an interview.

Adams was the only president who was also a published poet.

John Quincy Adams was the son of the second president, and he was the first president of whom a photograph exists.

John and Louisa raised silkworms at the White House.

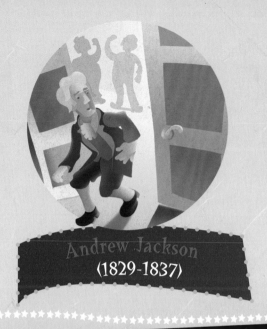

Andrew Jackson
(1829-1837)

After his inauguration, Andrew Jackson invited all of his old friends to the White House for a party. The party turned into a drunken brawl, and Jackson had to sneak out. He spent his first night as president in a hotel.

Jackson was the first president to ride on a train while in office.

The first attempt to assassinate a U.S. president was made on Andrew Jackson.

When President Jackson left the White House, he had only $90 in his pocket.

The town of Adams, New Hampshire, changed its name to Jackson after Andrew Jackson beat John Quincy Adams in the presidential race.

Andrew Jackson often ignored his official cabinet. Instead, he met with a bunch of his old friends in the White House kitchen. This group was called his Kitchen Cabinet. Some say they had more influence on the president than members of his official cabinet.

Indoor plumbing was put into the White House during Jackson's term. Before that, the presidents used outhouses.

Jackson's marriage caused a lot of controversy. His wife's divorce was not final, which meant that she was still legally married. Neither Jackson nor his wife knew this.

Jackson was a notorious fighter. While he was president, he had a bullet removed from his right arm from a fight that had occurred 20 years earlier. He still had a bullet in his left arm and another lodged next to his heart.

Martin Van Buren
(1837-1841)

Martin Van Buren was from Old Kinderhook, a small town in New York. His supporters formed the "OK Club" from the initials of his hometown. They also called him OK. Saying that Van Buren was OK meant that he was "all right." Over time, the term OK became part of everyday language.

Van Buren wrote an autobiography and never once mentioned his wife, to whom he was married for 12 years.

Van Buren was the first president to have police stationed at the White House.

When Van Buren was vice president of the Senate, he often felt like his life was in danger because of arguments over suggested laws. He always carried two loaded pistols for protection.

William Henry Harrison
(1841)

William Henry Harrison was the first president to die in office. His inauguration speech was the longest ever, at more than 8,400 words. Despite the bitterly cold weather at his inauguration, he insisted on giving the speech outside without a hat or coat. He later developed pneumonia, but he actually died of diarrhea while he was being treated.

Harrison was the only president who studied medicine, but he gave it up and became an officer in the Army.

Harrison was president for only 31 days. He did not make a single major decision during his term of office.

Harrison dropped out of college his senior year. The other seven members of his college class went on to hold high government positions, but he was the only one to become president.

Before John Tyler, no vice president had moved up to the presidency upon the death of a president. The Constitution was not clear about whether a vice president should simply act as president in case of a president's death or should succeed to the presidency. Tyler decided on the latter, setting the precedent for future successions. Some people called Tyler "His Accidency."

Tyler had the most children of any president—15. Eight were by his first wife, Letitia, and seven were by his second wife, Julia. The youngest child, Pearl, was born in 1861, when Tyler was 70.

Tyler was the first president to marry while in office.

The first impeachment proceedings ever to take place against a president began against Tyler in 1843 by those who believed that he had taken the presidency illegally. The congressional resolution to start the proceedings was not passed.

James Knox Polk
(1845-1849)

Sarah Polk did not like parties. She believed that serving alcoholic beverages at White House receptions was beneath the dignity of the president. Alcoholic beverages were strictly forbidden. Because of Sarah's strict rules, the music and dancing at President James K. Polk's inaugural ball were stopped when the presidential couple arrived. The music and dancing did not resume until after they had left.

Polk was the first full-term president not to seek re-election.

Polk was one of the most unexpected men to be elected as president. The delegates at the 1844 Democratic convention couldn't agree on one candidate, so they chose Polk out of desperation. The term "dark horse" was coined during this election. It referred to an unexpectedly nominated candidate. Polk won in one of the biggest upsets in presidential history.

It is said that Polk once had a gall bladder operation without anesthesia.

President Polk worked 12 to 14 hours a day in the White House. According to all evidence, Polk hated being president. He was so exhausted from his four years as president that he died just three months after leaving office.

Polk was the only Speaker of the House to later become president.

Zachary Taylor
(1849-1850)

At the time of his nomination for the presidency, Zachary Taylor had never even voted.

For one day, March 4, 1849, David Rice Atchison was acting president of the United States. Inauguration Day 1849 fell on a Sunday, and Zachary Taylor refused to be sworn in on the Sabbath. Therefore, until the following day when Taylor took the oath of office, Atchison, president of the Senate and next in line of succession, was technically the president.

Taylor died in office after serving only 16 months of his term. Doctors said that his death was the result of consuming huge quantities of iced milk and cherries after being out in the hot sun all day.

Taylor's wife lived in seclusion at the White House. At the time of Taylor's death, some people were surprised to learn of her existence.

Taylor was called "Old Rough and Ready." He was sloppy, cursed a lot, and chewed tobacco.

Millard Fillmore
(1850– 1853)

In 1851, Millard Fillmore and his cabinet helped fight a fire at the Library of Congress.

Fillmore's wife, Abigail, couldn't find a book in the White House when she arrived there as first lady. She acquired money from Congress and stocked the mansion with books, creating the first White House library.

When England's Oxford University wanted to present Millard Fillmore with an honorary degree, he refused it, feeling that he was not entitled to it.

Franklin Pierce
(1853-1857)

Two months before Franklin Pierce's inauguration, his son, Bennie, 12, was killed in a railroad accident. Before that, Pierce's other two children had died, one in infancy and another at the age of 4. Mrs. Pierce remained in seclusion for nearly two years and wore black every day, mourning for her dead children. She didn't attend her husband's inauguration, and the traditional Inaugural Ball was canceled.

Franklin Pierce was known as "Handsome Frank."

President Pierce was arrested for running down an elderly woman while driving his horse and carriage through the streets of Washington, D.C. Nobody pressed charges, and the case was closed.

Pierce's running mate, William Rufus De Vane King, took the oath of office in Cuba. However, he never made it to Washington. He returned to his home in Alabama and died shortly after the trip.

James Buchanan
(1857–1861)

The king of Siam presented a herd of elephants to James Buchanan as a gift.

Buchanan was the only bachelor president. He was once engaged, but his fiancée died.

Buchanan's niece, Harriet Lane, served as White House hostess for her bachelor uncle. He had raised her from the age of 9, when she was left an orphan. Harriet was very popular, much more so than her uncle, the president.

**Abraham Lincoln
(1861-1865)**

Abraham Lincoln carried letters, bills, and notes in his stovepipe hat.

Lincoln wore a black crepe band on his hat when he delivered the Gettysburg Address. The band was in memory of his son Willie, who had died nine months earlier.

Robert Lincoln, one of the president's sons, was at the scene of three presidential assassinations—his father's in 1865, James Garfield's in 1881, and William McKinley's in 1901.

Lincoln proclaimed Thanksgiving a national holiday in 1863.

Lincoln is still the tallest person to be president. He was 6 feet, 4 inches (193 cm).

Lincoln ran for the Illinois state legislature, the U.S. Senate twice, and U.S. vice president. He lost all of those races. But when he ran for U.S. president, he won.

An 11-year-old girl named Grace Bedell wrote Lincoln a letter saying he would look better with a beard. After he was elected, he let his beard grow and became the first president to have one. He kept his beard the rest of his life.

Lincoln was the first major leader in U.S. history to favor extending the vote to women.

Despite portrayals of Lincoln with a bass voice, he actually spoke in a piercing, high-pitched tone.

Lincoln believed in psychic powers. One week before he was shot, he had a dream about his death. The day of his assassination, he had another strange dream.

Andrew Johnson
(1865-1869)

Andrew Johnson never spent a day in school. Fellow workers in a tailor shop taught him the alphabet, and his girlfriend taught him to read and write.

Johnson was the first president to be impeached. The House of Representatives voted to impeach him for not following the Tenure of Office Act. However, Johnson was acquitted by one vote in the Senate and remained president.

Johnson was proud of his skill as a tailor. When he was governor of Tennessee, he made a suit for the governor of Kentucky. Johnson wore only suits that he custom-tailored himself.

Johnson was the only president to later become a U.S. senator after leaving the White House.

Johnson had a telegraph room installed in the White House.

Johnson was the first president to be visited by a queen.

Ulysses S. Grant
(1869–1877)

President Ulysses S. Grant was arrested in Washington, D.C., for speeding in his horse and carriage. The arresting officer was about to let him go when he recognized the president, but Grant insisted he do his duty.

Grant enjoyed painting in his free time.

Grant was the first West Point graduate to become president.

Grant was named Hiram Ulysses Grant. He didn't like that his initials were H.U.G., which spells *hug*. At West Point, he was mistakenly entered as "Ulysses Simpson Grant," and he left his name that way.

During Grant's administration, the yearly salary of the president doubled from $25,000 to $50,000.

Ulysses S. Grant smoked 20 cigars a day and died of throat cancer.

During the Civil War (1861–1865), cucumbers soaked in vinegar were a typical breakfast for Grant.

During his administration, President Grant established Yellowstone, the first national park in the United States.

Although President Grant was a great Civil War hero, he got queasy at the sight of rare meat and sick at the sight of blood.

The coldest Inauguration Day was in 1873, when Grant was sworn in as president for the second time. It was 4° F (minus 16° C).

Rutherford B. Hayes
(1877-1881)

The wife of Rutherford B. Hayes was the first person in the United States to own a Siamese cat.

Mrs. Hayes was also the first president's wife who was a college graduate.

Hayes was the first president to visit the West Coast.

President Hayes' wife, Lucy, didn't serve liquor in the White House. She became known as "Lemonade Lucy." She also didn't allow dancing, smoking, and card playing.

The title "first lady" was not used until Hayes' term. A popular play called *The First Lady of the Land* was produced about Dolley Madison. The press started calling Hayes' wife the first lady. The title has stuck ever since.

James A. Garfield
(1881)

James Garfield could write with both hands at the same time. Sometimes he wrote Greek with one hand and Latin with the other.

Garfield had a dog named Veto.

Garfield was the first left-handed president.

President Garfield may have foreseen his own death. Only a couple of days before he was shot, he sent for Robert Lincoln, the only surviving son of Abraham Lincoln. He asked Robert to go over every detail of his father's assassination. And only months before his own death, Garfield had taken out an insurance policy for $25,000.

Garfield was president for just 199 days. He was shot by Charles Julius Guiteau on July 2, 1881.

The public was concerned about the president's family after his death. They raised more than $300,000 for Mrs. Garfield and her children.

Chester A. Arthur
(1881-1885)

When Chester Alan Arthur, Garfield's vice president, suddenly became president, he refused to move into the White House until it had been thoroughly cleaned and refurnished.

Arthur personally supported the first Civil Service Act, which made it necessary to pass tests to get certain government jobs. It had been a disappointed office-seeker who had shot and killed President Garfield.

Arthur's secretary of war was Abraham Lincoln's son Robert.

Arthur had a French chef in the White House.

Grover Cleveland
(1885-1889, 1893-1897)

Grover Cleveland was the only president to marry in the White House. He wrote out the invitations himself. In the wedding ceremony, he had the word *obey* deleted from the bride's vows.

Cleveland was also the only president to serve two separate terms. He left the White House in 1889 and returned four years later for a second term.

Within a span of only three and a half years, Grover Cleveland had been mayor of Buffalo, New York, governor of New York, and president of the United States.

Cleveland was the first president to use fireworks at his inauguration.

President Cleveland had known his young wife from the day she was born. Her father had been Cleveland's law partner. At 21 years old, she was the youngest first lady ever.

Mrs. Cleveland was the first wife of a president to give birth to a child in the White House. The baby was Esther Cleveland.

The candy bar "Baby Ruth" is said to be named after Ruth, the youngest daughter of President Cleveland.

Cleveland was the only county sheriff to become a U.S. president.

President Cleveland enjoyed hunting and fishing. His favorite hunting rifle was called "Death and Destruction."

Benjamin Harrison
(1889–1893)

Benjamin Harrison's grandfather, William Henry Harrison, had also been president.

When electricity was installed in the White House during Benjamin Harrison's administration, the president's family often went to bed at night leaving all the lights on. Everyone was afraid to touch the switches.

President Harrison started the custom of flying the U.S. flag from public buildings.

John Scott Harrison, a farmer born in Indiana, was both the son and the father of a president. William Henry Harrison was his father, and Benjamin Harrison was his son.

Harrison was the last president to have a beard.

The first Christmas tree appeared in the White House during Harrison's administration.

Harrison made 140 speeches in 30 days during a tour and never repeated a single speech.

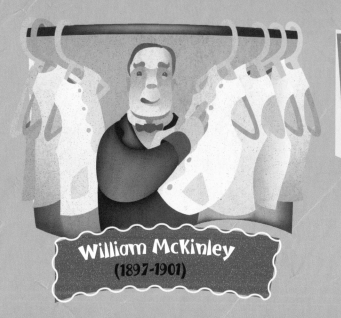

William McKinley
(1897-1901)

William McKinley was known for his spotless white vests. He changed into a clean one several times a day.

McKinley loved cigars but wouldn't allow himself to be photographed with one. He didn't want to set a bad example for the children of the country.

President McKinley always wore a lucky red carnation in his buttonhole. At an exposition in Buffalo, New York, after he had given his flower to a little girl in the crowd, an assassin shot him. He died eight days later from the wounds.

Theodore Roosevelt
(1901–1909)

The Roosevelt family had a one-legged chicken and a six-toed cat named Slippers.

Theodore Roosevelt's wife and mother both died on the same day, February 14, 1884.

Roosevelt loved to play with his children. Every member of the Roosevelt family had a pair of wooden stilts.

President Roosevelt got his face on Mount Rushmore because he was the favorite president of the sculptor who carved the faces.

Roosevelt was the first president and first American to win the Nobel Peace Prize.

In 1912, during a campaign to return to the presidency, Theodore Roosevelt was shot in an attempted assassination. The bullet lodged in his chest, but Roosevelt went on with his speech for 50 minutes. Afterward he went to a hospital, where the bullet was removed. A metal eyeglass case in his breast pocket had stopped it from going through to his heart, and he recovered quickly from the wound.

Roosevelt had once refused to shoot a bear cub while hunting, which inspired a political cartoon. The bear in the cartoon further inspired toy manufacturers, and the result was the "Teddy Bear." People began calling him "Teddy," which he didn't like. None of his friends or relatives called him that.

One day Roosevelt had a friendly boxing match with a young military aide. The president received a blow on his left eye that ruptured a blood vessel. By 1908, four years after the boxing incident, Roosevelt had completely lost the sight in his left eye. The secret was kept for years.

Glossary

acquitted—declared innocent of a crime or wrongdoing

administration—the period of time during which a government holds office

assassinate—to murder an important or famous person

autobiography—story of a person's own life written by that person

cabinet—a group of officials who give advice to the president

campaign—actions planned and carried out to bring about a particular result

candidate—a person who runs for office

delegate—a person who is chosen to act for others; a representative

Democratic convention—a large meeting during which a political party chooses its candidates

dissenting—a differing opinion

expedition—a journey made for a particular reason

impeachment—bringing formal charges of wrong conduct against a public official

inauguration—the ceremony of putting a person in office

indicted—accused and charged with committing a crime

legislature—a group of people in the U.S. government who have the power to make or pass laws

nomination—the choice of a person to run for office

running mate—the person a candidate is running with

seclusion—hidden from sight

senator—one of the 100 people in the Senate who make laws

Speaker of the House—leader of the House of Representatives and one of the most powerful offices in Washington, D.C.

succeeded—came after and took the place of

term—length in office

unanimously—showing total agreement

unopposed—without argument

veto—the power of the president, governor, or official group to keep something from being approved

West Point—the United States Military Academy

Index

To Learn More

At the Library

Pascoe, Elaine. *First Facts About the Presidents*. Woodbridge, Conn.: Blackbirch Press, 1996.

Phillips, Louis. *Ask Me Anything About the Presidents*. New York: Avon Books, 1992.

Provensen, Alice. *The Buck Stops Here: The Presidents of the United States*. San Diego: Browndeer Press, 1997.

Sobel, Syl. *Presidential Elections and Other Cool Facts*. Hauppauge, N.Y.: Barron's Educational Series, 2001.

On the Web

FactHound offers a safe, fun way to find Web sites related to this book. All of the sites on FactHound have been researched by our staff.

1. Visit *www.facthound.com*
2. Type in this special code: 1404837485
3. Click on the FETCH IT button.

Your trusty FactHound will fetch the best sites for you!

Look for all of the books in the Freaky Facts series:

Ancient Coins Were Shaped Like Hams and Other Freaky Facts About Coins, Bills, and Counterfeiting

Cows Sweat Through Their Noses and Other Freaky Facts About Animal Habits, Characteristics, and Homes

Earth Is Like a Giant Magnet and Other Freaky Facts About Planets, Oceans, and Volcanoes

Three Presidents Died on the Fourth of July and Other Freaky Facts About the First 25 Presidents

Your Skin Weighs More Than Your Brain and Other Freaky Facts About Your Skin, Skeleton, and Other Body Parts

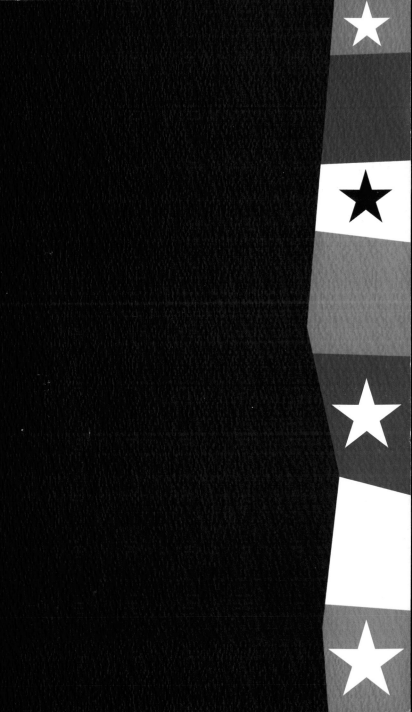